Eating a Cheeseburger During the End Times

Poems By John Grochalski

Kung Fu Treachery Press

Rancho Cucamonga, CA

Acknowledgments:

Some of these poems have appearing in the following publications: *Mad Swirl, The Rye Whisky Review, Peeking Cat Poetry, Duane's Poetree, The Stockholm Review, Under the Bleachers, Runcible Spoon, Live Nude Poems, As it Ought to be, Bradlaugh's Finger, Medusa's Kitchen, Red Shift, Spill Words* and *The Daily Drunk.*

TABLE OF CONTENTS

For Ally, who lives it too

*The greatest mystery about a human being is not his
reaction to sex or praise, but the manner in which he
contrives to put in twenty-four hours a day.*

-Sinclair Lewis

your wife's phone

when a cop calls
and he's using
your wife's phone
your first thought is
well, at least it's not a mugger
or some kind of serial killer
but then you realize
that you're talking to a cop
on your wife's phone
you think to ask where she is
why he's calling you
you do it all casual
like, *what'd that crazy lady do now, officer?*
but when he says
that she's been hit by a car
you think that's absurd
but i just texted her, you say
like ten minutes ago, you say
like the world couldn't possibly go
and let your wife get hit by a car
between the minutes of
6:25 PM and 6:35 PM
you ask if she's all right
because that's just instinct
and the cop says
that she's mobile
and you picture her on the street corner

pacing back and forth
yelling at cops and people
at the faceless bastard who hit her
but mobile just means that she's conscious
that her legs are moving
which is the first thing you see
your wife laying on her back
on the wet pavement
legs shaking from the cold
in the same clothing she was wearing
when you parted this morning
when you didn't think the evening
would begin with a cop calling
on your wife's phone
but there she is
and there you are calling for her
screaming, *who in the fuck did this?*
and you brush off some cop
who tries to grab you when you go to her
like a crime scene in a movie
and there are people everywhere watching
and there are cop cars
and there are ambulances
the street is a wet smear of blue and red lights
except the big white headlights
of an ambulance
parked in front of your wife
who hears your voice
who is calling to you
but doesn't look like she can really see you

and you, say, *baby, it's going to be all right*
but you don't know that yet
you've only known one person
who was ever hit by a car
and he fucking died
then a cop comes over to you
and gives you your wife's wallet
and her keys
and her brand-new bag
with the strap now broken
he asks you your name
and writes it down in some cop notebook
and you ask him,
who in the fuck did this?
and he says, *don't worry about that right now*
as the paramedics
start to put your wife on a stretcher
and she's calling to you
calling out your name
and you want to say to the cop
what do you mean don't worry about this right now?
even though he's already started to walk away
so you start to go toward your wife
but the cop turns around
and says,
oh, i almost forget
as he reaches inside his coat pocket
then hands you back
your wife's phone.

drunkard outside the E.R.
at one in the morning

he looks like
he's directing traffic
or in charge of all the cars idling

bald head and a manager's moustache

he has a blue blazer and carries his phone
like it's a walkie-talkie or something

only the whiff of whiskey
and his hospital wristband give him away

it's the same one
my wife is wearing
five hours in the E.R.
after being hit by a car in the snow and rain

he keeps saying, loco
like *everything* is loco

getting hit by a car
a broken collarbone
and a stack of medical papers to boot

or standing outside an E.R.
in the pitch black of a new day

hungry and exhausted and shivering

as the rain turns to snow
then back to rain again

watching the drunkard outside the E.R.
at one in the morning
stumble all over the street
waving his phone at buses and black sedans

king of the phantoms
until the DT's kick in

and everything truly
is loco here, man,

just fucking loco.

the gamblers

the football coverage
on the three huge televisions
seems loud and endless

and we've chosen bad seats
near where the betting pools are resting
on the glossy wooden bar

men keep coming in to hover over them
dropping five for a pint
and another twenty on an unused box
they crowed us
as they take pictures of the spread
making it hard to find some personal space

they look like fat ansel adamses
in tight football jerseys and fitted hats

taking landscape shots
at every available angle

of warped paper and smudged sharpie numbers

sending texts to the ones
who have yet to make it out of their homes

the bartender points to the spread
and asks me if i'm in it for the game
or do i want some action?

i want to tell him
that i put all my chips in
on the promise of a quiet lunch
and a few colds pints
in a dead bar on a sunday afternoon

but that has failed to come to fruition

instead i just tell him
that i'm not a betting man

as more of the gamblers file in
trying to turn their paycheck money
into temporary bliss

so they can maybe avoid the real gamble here

the one of trying to make it
in a country week by week

that tries so hard
to have its big fat stack of capitalist cards

forever set
to work
against
you

a country that turns us all into gamblers

no matter what we want
to sit there and think.

these chicken wings don't run

the back
of the waiter's t-shirt
has a tattered american flag on it
and it says

if you love america
you'll love this bar

but if i'm sitting in here
then surely the two ideas can't be intertwined

i don't love america

to tell the truth
i don't really like this bar

with its american flags everywhere
and its corny fallen military hero motif

ten television sets
half of them set to ESPN
the other half set to Fox News

and every table and bar stool
full of doughy white dudes
dressed like they're off to the big game
or set for a nazi rally

no, i don't like this place
but i love their buffalo wings

and i'm so hungry
for all i care
the waiter could be wearing a t-shirt
with uncle sam's sinister, stupid tired-ass
glaring back at me

one menacing, geriatric finger
painted electric orange and dripping goodness

pointing at me
as if to say

listen, you commie wimp
these here chicken wings

they sure as shit
don't fucking run

which means
i can fake being a patriot
at least until my belly is full

and i could swallow lady liberty whole
if she came waltzing on in here
dressed only in hot sauce.

duncan

duncan is running around the kettle bar
with his sister olive

they are screaming and yelling

while people are
starting in early on the day's drunk

duncan is three and vacant
olive is pushing two at best

she has a set of pipes on her
that could raise the dead

there are no other children in the bar
because it's a *bar*

duncan's old man is your garden variety domestic asshole

with his receding hairline and dad gut
hidden under a faded football jersey

he apologies to my wife and i
when duncan and olive smack into our stools
for the third time

but he doesn't mean it

because his america counts more than mine

dad is enjoying his stolen afternoon beer
with his bros too much
to worry about duncan and olive
killing other people's time

he's too caught up in the entitlement of being a parent

to see his kids
for the screaming creeps they are

because duncan and olive are so precious
their shit doesn't stink

they're the zenith of what he'll accomplish in this world
other than watching another NFL season

ignorance that he'll pass on
like family jewels and disease

boutique named monsters free to run around a bar

screaming and yelling
and raising holy hell on a monday afternoon

like they're at a playground in a park

duncan in his rookie-of-the-year t-shirt
olive in her plaid dress

smacking their heads off the worn bar

olive screaming bloody murder
duncan prat falling and farting

the bartender giving us free shots in apology

as dad of the year
gets up to take a piss

but not before
he comes over to the bar

and orders all of his bros
another blessed round.

watching two boys double-team a third
on a sunny afternoon in the park

assembly line violence
tastes like candy on stolen land

and to the victors
will go the devil's spoils
and bragging rights to last an hour

and what is that smell in the air?

blood?
the coming of spring?

i am reminded
of many things
watching this donnybrook unfold
from tomfoolery
into an unfair game of cat and mouse

mostly that to make a proper fist
you need to keep your thumb untucked

that i need to stop at the liquor store
for both vodka *and* wine

how youth is fleeting

there's no shame in running away
from the obtuse and absurd

and that when i was growing up
i almost always preferred

the boys who played with dolls.

the great migration

fresh from
a public restroom bath

homeless joe
sits on the bench
picking the remaining lice
out of his hair

holding one squirming specimen
up to the white light of the sun

as all the clean cops
circle him cautiously

and the rest
of the good citizens

grab their precious belongings

to move
from here to there

a diaspora of
the lucky and well-possessed

fucking off to somewhere else.

as two boys kick a ripe tomato
down the garbage-strewn sidewalk

i wonder what the hunger rates
in the united states of america are

surely, they're pretty high
or the food bank would've stopped sending me mail

i feel shame over the uneaten salad
sitting there waiting to be thrown out
in my work refrigerator

the victim of two spontaneous slices of pizza
the thumbed nose at food i'm supposed to eat at forty-
whatever

i stop to consider
which fruit and vegetable stand
those boys got the tomato from

which merchant lost at capitalism today
or decided to turn sustenance into sport
to appease two restless boys

i think maybe
i should be the adult here
in this scenario

pull the boys away from their fun
to tell them all about starving kids

in china
in ethiopia
in parts of brooklyn they'll never see

tell them
back in my days we kicked real balls

but that would seem judgmental of me
or at the very least racist
and maybe somewhat homophobic

and there's enough of that
going around here these days

plus, you never know
whom you're going to offend

what poverty of pocket or mind
that lead to kicking a tomato for sport

also there's still the issue
of my own uneaten salad

all of the uneaten salads that i've spurned
then later tossed away in silent shame

left to rot away
in a mound of garbage
shipped somewhere upstate

guilts that have lasted me decades
culinary hypocrisies blasting like fireworks

over a glittering trash heap
on the fourth of july.

a poem of gray clouds on a fucked evening

-after li po

the red faces of traffic on 75th street
and kids shouting invective in the park

…in both, there is no lack of bullshit
and violence

as the gray clouds follow me
back to the liquor store
on another fucked evening

where dignity and my liver
are the cost of making it work

here in bootstrap america.

post-wine katezenjammer

only i'm back
in the booze store again
buying another two magnum bottles of red

and a plastic jug of vodka to boot

and the guys who work there
are huddled around the cash register talking
ignoring me and not taking my money

i've become a fixture here like the floor

they are talking about katarina
and why she quit so suddenly

conflicted with her college schedule
couldn't hack retail

she took up nannying, one of them says

i wish she'd nanny me!

and they all laugh
and make sex noises

and somewhere in america
katarina's ears are ringing

to the dull hum of the patriarchal void

as i stand there with the two wine bottles
the jug of vodka
and a crumpled, miserable jackson in my hand

my hangover like the booze store's mascot

an afterthought
to their sexism

and fine-tooled misogyny.

cracks on the sidewalk

in america
there is money for endless war

money to put immigrants in detention forever
and keep kids in cages

money rolling over money rolling
from sea to shining sea
into the hands of greedy pigs

money flying over broken neighborhoods
at thirty-thousand feet

a gilded carbon imprint

money for alarms
for gated communities
so they don't have to deal with the peasants

dark money to be made off of elections
lobbying dollars suffocating the constitution

money to keep nutbags
up to their stomachs in firearms and fat

but where's the motherfucking coin
to fix this crack on the sidewalk?

the one that cost me ten bucks
when i tripped over it
and dropped my bottle of wine?

its blood-red bounty
swirling right into the sewer
and gone forever

where's the money for that america?

because it sure as fuck
isn't sitting here in my wallet.

spring, i come home to the port a potty
gone from in front of my living room window

the blue box
with that fun, bouncy name, callahead

gone

the one that the construction guys
used during the day

that the neighborhood men used at all hours

but what of the delivery guys
once again forced into doing their pee-pee dance?

or the work bros in cool guy shades
who pulled their sports cars of loud rap bass
right in front of my living room window

where will they go to take that unexpected rush hour shit?

old men with weak bladders?
the cocksure young locking lips inside on a dare?

the homeless men on quixotic quests
never again experiencing their eureka moment

or the packs and packs of sweaty guys
coming home from basketball in the park

who stood in stadium long lines
laughing and shouting, talking about their pricks

men always men
slamming and slamming the shitter door

as i sat on my living room couch
watching them and taking in the stench

drowning out the night in vodka
and the mercy and the power
of loud rock'n'roll

good lord what will happen to us all?

for the lady i met in the laundry room

let us speak
less of our fate
and more to the fact
that the laundry must be done

we are both slaves
to societal norms and clean underwear

but does that mean we need to discuss the weather?

or the old building superintendent
who let the cockroaches
roam as free and wild as buffalo
in old western stories?

six years after the fact
talk about beating your proverbial dead horse!

the way his ears must ring to this day!

and don't you know your ancient grudge
does nothing for your eyes under these dim laundry lights?

besides, i could tell you tall tales
about the new superintendent

we could sing psalms beneath
the corroded water-damaged plaster of my bedroom ceiling

be watered tortured
with the way my shower drips

have our very confidence in humanity
shook to its core
with the way his, screaming monster child
runs past my window
caught in the thralls of liquid bubbles
and street chalk

or how his wife stares voodoo daggers into me
whenever i offer up a small complaint

let us instead
turn this moment of drudgery and chore
into silence

human beings are akin to angels
when they are silent and otherwise involved

let's leave the conversation to the gnats
that have begun to congregate in this building anew

so that when we finish
we can part ways the best of strangers

and i can go back to my apartment
of sound mind

and not have to tell my poor wife

that the crazy, loquacious old bat in 2C
is at it again.

alone, i pour another double vodka

and let marvin gaye
permeate the living room

to drown out the upstairs neighbor

whose feet thunder across the floor
like she's unfurling the wrath of zeus

tonight it sounds
as if she's rolling bowling balls across her floor
then running across the wood

to roll them back

and i really shouldn't
be drinking double vodkas this way
at my age

it disrupts the sleep
and my brain is dodgy these days

but we do as we must to get by

and, besides, if i stopped now
it would be a lifetime of false, sober smiles

given to bowling ball people
living bowling ball lives

rolling and rolling all over me

trapping me in an oubliette of pleasantries
with no rusty blade in my hand

to cut the occasional vein
and let it all bleed.

hungover and awakening
to the neighbor's asshole dog

hungover and awakening
to the neighbor's asshole dog

staring at me
then barking at me
as i lift kitchen blinds

coffee-less
with the scent of stale vodka and wine
burning my nostrils

my head a cartography
of potholes and fill-in-the-blanks
from the previous evening

the way it stands there
bouncing
yapping
cold black eyes
white muppet face

owning my aural landscape
until it condescends to forget me
and take its shit

the mutt's owner

shrugging down an apology
while playing on his cell phone

i shut the blind
and return myself
into the pale gray blue
of lightless linoleum

and know
that while not all humans
commit murder

all humans must surely understand
the pure pleasure involved

in murderous intent.

spring in my heart, on my mind
as, hungover, i walk up heart attack hill

a sky of sun
and no clouds

and inevitably
some well-meaning dullard
will tell me that today is a good day

and expect the same sentiment
from me in return

spring in my heart, on my mind
as, hungover, i walk up heart attack hill

and the incline
never seems to end

there is a good chance
that this could be my last journey

huffing and having to stop for air
my heart thumping in my chest

the scent of tulips
mixing with last night's wine
on my breath

the acid in my stomach
doing a cartwheel

but to be drunk again and at home
with the lights off and the blinds drawn

rather than subject myself to this!

the joggers in their credit card clothing
and little brats on bikes

dogs barking love songs to america
as their owners pick up shit with smiles

the cartoon ideal

it would be almost worth it
to bite the big one right here

and never show up at my fucking job

only, in death,

i'd be without the memory
of the looks on all of their faces

that my demise would shit
on the polished cars and manicured lawns

of their oh-so-perfect day.

crossing the 72nd street foot bridge

the chinese women
walk slowly
in front of me

laughing as they read sex graffiti
tiptoeing over broken bottles

as i daydream vodka and wine
and the tenants of independent wealth

they twirl their blue and yellow
IKEA umbrellas

like cabaret stars

but then quietly pass the man
who's always drinking his beer
out of a can hidden in a paper bag

this is the after-work world in mid-may

in a moment when there is no rain
in a spring that could only be described

as deluge

crossing the 72nd street foot bridge
the rush hour traffic idles below us

as always, volcanic in its fury

the rumbling of engines
the honking of horns

a symphony of thunder
seemingly ready the strike us off our path
and combust

but still going nowhere
for miles and miles

in both directions.

the people in the grocery store
look like death warmed over

spoiled vegetables
and rancid meat

are what we get for a long day of servitude

long lines
and bored cashiers
playing on cell-phones

self-check machines
for the post-industrial world dandy

flat soda
and stale bread

warm beer by the caseload
that we'll drink to insanity and bliss

the people in the grocery store
look like death warmed over

coming home from work

to their common miseries
and their self-inflicted wounds

microwaved leftovers
and the dread faces of loved ones

rank capitalists bound and gagged

i hate them
as i hate myself

for making each other
suffer this way.

helping margaret in 5G

margaret in 5G
took me for a potential rapist
one time in the laundry room

now, she's rapping on my door with her cane
because she can't get her ass
back up to her own apartment

when i open my door
she's sweat-soaked and confused

margaret says, grab my bags,
what's the matter with you?

i grab them all like we're both coming home
from a fun day of shopping in the city

margaret says, get behind me, god damn it
so i don't fall

and for five flights
we take it one step at a time
in the sweltering sludge of summer

by the fifth floor i feel like shit
i can smell the wine and vodka
coming through my nostrils and my pores

i stop because i feel like i'm going to pass out

what are you, a cripple? margaret says,
turning back to me

which i guess is better than a rapist

when we get to her door
margaret points to a corner

she says, put my damn bags there
for christ's sake, you milquetoast

so i do

then margaret says,
i hope you know i'm not
giving you any money for this

then she grabs up all her shit
like she's hercules

sniffs and says,
hey, you're nothing but a drunk

and then slams her door.

kay's clothing shop

kay's clothing shop
on fifth avenue, downtown pittsburgh

where old men tailored garments
with pins in their mouths

smelling of after shave
and whatever they had for breakfast

my dad said this was how
you bought pants in his day

but i knew the truth to our annual visits

i knew that we were in kay's because i was too fat
for my parents to buy me school pants off of the retail rack

because i couldn't control what i put in my mouth
because i ate and ate and ate and ate when i wasn't even
hungry

because there was an unexplainable void to fill
and i was hell-bent on filling it, like i do with booze now

so we had to come down here to kay's
where i was the youngest person in the store

to have old men pull polyester pants off of racks
in the dullest of colors

navy blue and gray and shit brown

how i'd try them on with tears in my eyes
an appreciative smile on my face

embarrassed for myself and my family

as the old men fiddled
with my waist and legs
and made measurements

to my inseam and legs
to have the pants taken out at the waist

as i daydreamed
the fast-food cheeseburger and fries
i'd get afterwards

or what it would feel like
to show up at school on that first day

thin and free
and just like everyone else

my god, for once
just like everyone else.

eighth grade desk

the nun toppled my desk
and made me carry its contents
around in a garbage bag for a week

to show me how messy i was

to show me that cleanliness
was next to godliness

and that i was closer in kin
to the devil than that

and i think about her this morning
thirty some years later

her cold, pious flesh
rotting under six feet of earth

as i sit here surrounded

by loose change in crooked piles
and stacks of yellowing paper

dust on my bookshelves

last night's clothing on the floor
to be worn again today

my breath full of sleepiness and old wine

happier than a pig in shit
that the devil came calling for me back then

before her lousy god ever could.

grape drink and snuff

once as a kid

i made jackson pollock
splatters of purple chunks
on the hot pavement

i made getting sick an art

walking home in a daze
under the blistering sun

throwing up
throwing up

the latch key kid of the avant garde

half a dozen cartons of grape juice
and a bottom lip full of mint-flavored snuff

for lunch

as the neighbor lady asked me if i was all right

and i wanted to tell her
that those free summer camp kids
who thought they had my fat boy number

those prince and princesses
of this tin-shack suburb

could never tell me that i wasn't solid
that i didn't live up to my potential

that i was art
as royal as they came

but instead
i spewed up my genius
in violet hues

all over the concrete again.

frank fanello played guitar

like clockwork
every time us kids
came out onto the *cul de sac*
with a wiffle ball and bat
or a nerf football

frank fanello played guitar

he brought out his black electric
with a portable amp

and an extension cord
that he plugged into a jack in his garage

then frank stood there on his driveway
in front of his big, blue station wagon

playing
led zeppelin
jimi hendrix

the star-spangled banner over and over

he kept our wiffle balls
if they went into his yard

held the balls out to us to see who'd try and grab them

frank called us punks and wimps
tossed the balls into his garage
and went back to playing clapton

older neighbors said he was crazy

rumor had it that frank killed
his girlfriend's dog back in the 60's

he once told us kids
that he used to drop children out of airplanes
back in vietnam

frank was a noted draft dodger

one time
he chased his wife
around their yard
with a steak knife

frank grabbed her
and put the knife in her hands

and yelled, do it, go ahead and do it, you coward

that was a crazy memorial day weekend

crazy like how
frank fanello played guitar
every time we played ball

how he stood there on his driveway
back arched and knees bent

like he was playing guitar
in madison square garden

instead of on a dead-end street
in the pittsburgh suburbs

antagonizing a bunch of kids
because he had nothing better to do

kids who hated him
who hated his guitar

kids who'd let frank know
just how much he was despised

with rotten vegetables
shaving cream and eggs

on those nights
when the sun went down
and the street got quiet

when frank fanello
was so tired from playing guitar

that he forgot
to put his big, blue station wagon

back inside the garage.

ridiculous male bravado

boys
used to have these standoffs
in high school

we'd go to some undisclosed location
like a bus stop or the park

the combatants would stand face to face
glare and try to look hard

maybe one pushed the other
and the other pushed back

to tell the truth they looked scared
like they didn't want to hurt anyone or get hurt

but were caught up in this ridiculous male bravado

kill or be killed in america

there were never any girls there
they were off being told a different kind of lie

after about fifteen minutes of this sideshow
all the hoopla began to die down

the fighters couldn't remember
what they were mad about anyway

and one by one
we walked away from the stalled melee

slinking back into our own
little internal dramas

pacifists anew.

hungover and exhausted with all of this i put
down the cell phone and listen as kids play
video games

sitting
in this barely air-conditioned room
full of children i'm duty-bound to protect

i play on my cell phone
like every other dullard

and try not to envision the big picture
try not to examine the life

but it's hard

back in pittsburgh last weekend
my old man told me
that i needed to start getting my prostate checked

prepare for the big colon exam at fifty

as if fifty
was just another benchmark
in this endgame played by one

and not some train
careening off the rails
and coming straight for me

it's too much this aging

counting down
seconds, minutes, hours and days

encapsulating decades within the minutiae
of casual conversation between old friends

existence itself can drive you mad
when you try and search for lost time

hungover and exhausted with all of this
i put down the cell phone and listen as kids play video games

and giggle
and laugh with youthful abandon
and run around the room
touching things that i should be telling them
to leave well enough alone

for a moment i hate them all

sit envious
with how their child-hours seem to loiter

as if their little long lives
won't suddenly catch on fire like mine

and this march of time
won't ever happen to them

the good samaritan

the sound of pre-teen boys
exchanging curses over video games
in this small kafka room

is my existential dread
in exchange for a paycheck

if i were a masochist
i'd send my sworn enemies in here
so that they could swoon over my fate

sensing my eternal damnation
he comes waddling over to me

grubby, maybe eleven years old

he opens a fresh bag of cheetos
under these fluorescent hell lights

points the tip
of its fiery orange embers my way

and says, come on, come on, bro
take as many as you want.

ghosts of summer

give me back
the smack of wiffleball bat
on wiffleball

the home run kings of cul de sacs
surrounding duplex houses

playing 10-run rule

or until it was all decided
when the wiffleball went rolling down the sewer

give me back
playing nerf football in the shade
with concrete gods

making star wars action figure plots
right out of the humid, sweltering air

the sun-sick joy of evermore romance
that wouldn't last a week

trading baseball cards on picnic benches
like sweaty stock brokers fearing a crash

those suburban kids
those suburban girls

those ghosts of summer
playing tag with the streetlights and fireflies

some of whom have died too young
some of whom have lived
to grow as gray as i

oh, give me back that freedom
of faux innocence and blissful indecision

you petrifying wretch of time.

salsa dancing on the subway platform

she thinks she's bad
she thinks she's the shit

salsa dancing on the subway platform
at rush hour on the way home

in her tight turquois pants
and a white blouse that can no longer hold her tits

she thinks she's the sexiest thing here
and she might just be right

one hand on her belly
the other raised like she's pledging allegiance

hot pink lipstick
and gold hoop earrings

moving at the hips
bending at the knees

swaying her ass against the cold brick wall

if only her moves
could make this train come quicker.

the patriot

sleeping on the
evening subway train

his legs spread like canyons

sitting there
taking up two seats

with a t-shirt
tight over his fat belly

emblazoned with old glory

and a phrase that says
i stand for the flag

as the pregnant woman
hovering over him

daydreams america
and a cure for sore feet.

block party USA

overheard
the sky is gray
as the deluge comes

just like the television weather forecaster
in the mini skirt said it would

rain all day

and all of their american flags hang limp

their colors dulled
against the lead pencil sky

as the
god fearing
country loving
patriots

sit on their stone porches
with bored, disappointed, scowling faces

while the dogs on the block walk around
sniffing each other's asses

getting gleefully soaked in the rain

listening to neighborhood idiots shoot off
fireworks while i get drunk on warm red wine

and think
nationalism is a lot like
the american workplace

simultaneously farcical and punitive

that is to say
i'd like to lay down the law
on these idiots who've been at it for hours

blowing shit up and then whooping about it

while the dogs around here
wallow in fear and madness

the starlings drop dead from trees

it never gets old to them
these seasonal patriots

memorial day to labor day

i wonder where
this kind of zest and tenacity
would be of real benefit to the nation

i've been reading a lot
about infrastructure problems lately

and maybe a few of these jokers could
put all of that energy into building bridges

or at least fix the potholes on this street

but there i go being silly again

listening to neighborhood idiots
shoot off fireworks
while i get drunk on warm red wine

is a national pastime of its own

sitting here with the blinds drawn
waiting on tomorrow

when it'll be nothing
but burn marks on the pavement
and firecracker casings strewn like confetti

dogs with PTSD
out for their morning shit

as i get out of bed with a hangover
and stare into the bathroom mirror

bearded and strung out

thinking that i look
like good ol' uncle sam

or maybe something else
just as coldly moronic and sinister.

american groupthink and apple pie

it happened
at school pep rallies mostly
or on the school bus
going to the football game

the dozens
or the hundreds of them breaking into
school chants
or battle cries
then usa! usa! usa!

sounding like ravenous nazis on the prowl

you could only look around
in fear and wonder

at their red faces
the spittle coming out of their mouths
their fists moving like hammers

the blind capitulation
to conformity

american groupthink and apple pie

as they chanted the same doggerel
over and over again
like it was coming from their hearts

so it is no wonder
to see them all now as adults

pasty-faced and flabby
fat from the heartland

the mendacity of exceptionalism on stolen land

still chanting
but this time for crooked politicians

still caught up
in the same stupid orthodoxy

that has kept them
shackled to the many

the very blood and soil
that has been strangling
the essence of their humanity

since birth.

red meat

america separates
families at the border

america puts kids in cages
and leaves them there for years

america eats too much red meat
red meat for breakfast, lunch and dinner

it eats red meat shaped like bombs
while it kills itself at thankless jobs

and watches too much television

america watches kids
living in cages on television

in between commercials
for big cars and more red meat

gets drunk and jerks off to torture porn

then it gets on its knees
and prays for freedom and the love of god

before america
wraps itself up snug in the american flag

and puts its bloated body
full of red meat and disease

to bed.

to the cockroach still alive
and stuck alone on a trapper max glue pad
in the basement of my job

you'll get no sympathy from me
moving your antennae from side to side

anxious and confused at your fate

i'm just glad that you're not
one of the merciless rank and file
that i have to kill at home

like it's a second fucking job

brethren who have defiled
my coffee pot and toaster

sat on walls and scoffed at me in the bathroom
when i'm helpless taking an early morning shit

run roughshod on my kitchen floor

you carry no communicable diseases
i'll give you that

damn the mosquitos, right?

but to the cockroach still alive

and stuck alone on a trapper max glue pad
in the basement of my job

i say die
you son-of-a-bitch

die all day and night

and if i wasn't already late
getting back from my afternoon break

i'd stand over you
like some jailhouse executioner

watching passionless
until your insect nazi ass
was good and gone.

card shop carl

card shop carl
is excited to see me
whenever i come in the card shop door

i used to be suspicious of carl
but have since learned to live
with his exuberance and adulation

card shop carl is
tattooed and scrawny and haggard

he's been to rehab a few times
and looks like he's endured some other tough shit

he brings up his years in the military a lot

carl was stationed in berlin in the 80's
so berlin is touchstone for him

everything that ever happened
that was any good in carl's life
happened in berlin

the booze
the women
tripping on LSD in kreutzberg

driving 160 km on the autobahn
while fucked up on pills

card shop carl's bucket list
is to get back to berlin

he likes to talk about rock and roll
and the writing of the beat generation

carl goes through all of the dead shows he's seen
while i look through baseball cards

tells me, *you should've seen jerry, man*

card shop carl talks so much
sometimes i lose track
of the cards i'm going through
or the money that i'm going to spend

once i ended up spending fifty bucks

most of my paycheck goes to the card shop
the other half goes to the liquor store

so i have to maintain a financial balance

card shop carl is off the sauce
we don't talk about the booze

unless the drinking happened
somewhere cool in berlin

card shop carl laughs and says to me,
what are we doin' man?

and i don't know how to answer

he's fifty-five and works in a baseball card shop
i'm forty-six and still buy baseball cards

to the untrained eye
we're either men of grand delusions
or men of immaculate leisure

in reality
we're men whose best years
are starting to get left behind

so i let carl talk
as i sift through cards

try and get out of the store
without spending another fifty

pretend to be fulfilled
by my conspicuous consumption

like carl is his berlin memories

and the wonderful silence
of momentary anonymity

as i head toward my other friends
at the local liquor store.

sunset park

little cops
drive their little cop vans
through sunset park
in the morning
collecting the men
standing around in small circles
doing nothing
but being latino

they collect the men
one by one

small conversations
slap on the cuffs

then the little cops
drive their little cop vans
out of sunset park
without so much as stopping
to look at manhattan
glittering
in the distance
like an untouchable jewel

in all that splendid summer sun.

miss morality police approximately

she makes herself a good neighbor
by loitering and shouting out into the void
like it's always noon

votes republican

stands for the flag
kneels for the cross

says kids these days have no morality

what with the…
and the…
and their…

then spouting off a list of juvenile inanities
that plague each successive generation
as it grows older and out of the zeitgeist's glance

it gets pretty boring down here in summer

trying to live a life between
heat waves, street festivals and parades

she has to do something to entertain herself

today she's the morality police

tomorrow it'll be smiling abject racist
in line at the over-priced grocery store

telling her buddy waiting behind her
how she's able to discern the good ones from the bad

just like the little arab girl
ringing up her groceries

who never flinches when she speaks

oh no
not even once.

what i should've said when the liquor store clerk
asked me if i was going to the neighborhood
summer festival

the word festival
means asshole in russian, i believe

there are too many cops standing in cop rows
with cop smirks on their cop faces

they won't let you drink beer on the street
…probably because of the cops

there are too many people
wearing t-shirts with the american flag on them

too many toddlers
waving american flags at cops

there are too many american flags in general

and i need to imagine something more tonight
than american flags and cops and summer festivals
and fireflies and humid summer nights
and pale-faced rapist boys chasing pale-faced girls

i'm going to get blind, stinking drunk
and sing the temptations at the top of my lungs

until my upstairs neighbor
comes home from the neighborhood summer festival

and pounds down on my ceiling
so hard that the plaster begins to fall.

orchestra of the damned

the new neighbors next door
like to move their furniture around
all day and night

there is always a pushing and shoving
and slamming of something
coming from their apartment

that rattles my walls

they have a newborn baby
who cries and cries ad nauseam too

the upstairs neighbor
likes her tv and her rap music loud

she pounds around in her cement shoes
until bits of plaster
cascade down onto my hardwood floor

while outside my window

the neighbors stop
to let their barking dogs do their business
jawing about neighborhood gossip

as cars roar by with custom built exhaust pipes
like we're in the pit at NASCAR

the delivery men come
with food and amazon packages

letting their cars idle with bass

dodging the panting joggers
and con men shouting into cell phones

amidst the garbage men
and jackhammers of construction

that reach me
sitting helplessly on the couch

like a symphony of shit
conducted by the devil

played so fluidly
by an orchestra of the damned.

bloody knuckles

bloody knuckles
and i am hungover again

sitting here
with my balls hanging out of
ripped boxer shorts

working on a headache
and a burning stomach

bloody knuckles
and i didn't even get them
from something good

like a bar fight
or a fight with a neighbor over some triviality

got them making the bed
smacking my hand
off the old, weathered box spring

bloody knuckles
and all i can do
is drink wine and vodka on the couch
with band aids on

watch the hours pass
through a broken tv

until i can go to bed
and sleep the wretched restless sleep
of the damned

maybe dream that i'm some
big time prizefighter

instead of just a clumsy drunk

who can't even properly make
his goddamned bed.

sunday afternoon paranoia in skinflint's bar

the bartender here thinks he knows me

every time i come in this joint
he looks at me and says, the *usual?*

like he's got some kind of keen insight
into the very center of my soul

that he and only he
knows just what i need

taking a pull on my first draft
i think to myself

that this afternoon
is the last afternoon
i'm ever coming in here

and no matter how good the service
i'll drop my money somewhere else

walk by this joint
and never look inside

leave mr. smug bartender prognosticator
to wonder sometimes

how our once close relationship
all went so very wrong.

arriving at work
to the homeless man who smells like urine

he sits on the stoop
like a sickly shroud
smelling faintly of urine

he's huddled in black

black suitcase
black duffle bag at his side

his face ghostly and pale
his lips white with kidney failure

sometimes there is a beer bottle or two at his side

he sits there shivering
as people walk by going to work
with huge coffees and bagel sandwiches
and little rolly bags trailing them like dogs

in less than twenty minutes
i will let him inside
where he will find a chair and read or sleep

until he pisses himself anew
the good people complain
and i have to ask him to leave

arriving at work
to the homeless man who smells like urine

sometimes i think about
how glad i am that i'm not him

but sometimes i think about
how the only real choices in america
are to work like a dog until you're half-dead
or to end up smelling like piss in the street

how everyone in this shithole nation
is just a few bad mondays
from being just like this guy

a few bad breaks
and america will throw you away
like trash

then i go inside
and i sit at my desk in the dark
with my head buried in my hands

and i wait for something better
that will never come.

my anxiety overwhelms

my anxiety overwhelms
it takes up a room and holds everyone hostage

it is a map of rosacea on my face
the rapid twitch of my eye

hundreds of pictures of my oven on my phone

it is checking faucets over and over again
never believing the sound of a locked door

my anxiety is christmas lights in october
it is snowfall in the spring
and a picnic in the driving rain

it is misdirected anger and frustration
at the ones that i love

it is not feeling loved but desperately alone

my anxiety is a thousand nights of hangovers

it is sitting on the couch next to me
begging another goddamned drink

it will never be good enough for anyone
and no one will ever be good enough for it

it will never believe you
no matter what you say

my anxiety could shoot someone on fifth avenue
and get away with it

if only my anxiety could hold a gun

instead it will come up with one hundred different scenarios
and none of them have to be true

but my anxiety will believe every single one
as if they are gospel

it will keep me up at night worrying
alive like a suicide
just for the sake of worrying

my anxiety will ruin:

vacations
your birthday
my birthday
dinners
lunches
weekends
movies
lovemaking
car rides
shopping

politics
hours
days
weeks
months
years

it will take a holiday and gleefully tell it to go to hell

my anxiety is strong enough to move mountains
but it would rather shake me to the core

and leave me hollow and scared
aching to fill myself back up
with anything

that i hope won't drag me back down
like an anchor into the cold gray ocean

my anxiety overwhelms

sometimes, i think
this is what it feels like

when it feels like death.

autumn, i come home to dog shit
littered all over my sidewalk

there are piles of it
laid haphazardly all over the sidewalk

mounds of dog shit
down the length of the block

one wonders if someone in my building
did this on purpose to spite my super

to thwart and frustrate him

because the hallways are filthy
and the cockroaches have come back

i don't think the super even cares

i can hear him laughing at the tv
behind his closed door

already unburdened
by the day's anxieties and fears

cockroaches
the furthest thing from his mind

and his soul

not yet willing

to center its entire self

around
somebody else's
shit.

i plumber

bleary-eyed
with poet words
forming in my head

i hold
a soaking wet plunger
over the toilet
at 4:45 a.m.

momentarily victorious

but as the water gurgles
and prepares to surge forward

i curse the very soul
of the superintendent
of this building

anew.

a regal man

he sits across from me
fidgeting during another train delay

and then he is gone

moments later
people are running by me

as if someone on this stalled train
has unleashed a plague

my wife looks back
then she gets up

pulling me
saying, just go

but i look back anyway

and there he is in a corner
my old fidgeting friend

squatting over a newspaper

shitting on the d train to manhattan
on a sunday afternoon

the stench is horrid

people are holding their noses
holding their mouths

i can't look away

i'm floored by the audacity
i'm shamed by his uncontrollable need

the power our bodies have
over our will is astounding

i watch him finish and get up

hiking up his pants
tucking in his shirt
buckling his belt

picking up the soiled newspaper and folding it
like he's saving some parts for later

standing there alone
at the opposite end from everyone

a regal man, for sure
as our stinking train rolls into the station

where he gets off and joins
the rapidly moving crowd

just as common and unassuming

as me
and you
and everybody else

going about their day.

young women eating tacos

young women eating tacos

spilling tortilla
lettuce, tomato and meat

all over the pavement

still look elegant

licking sour cream
and hot sauce off of their fingers

to the young men
calling after them

as they messily strut
down the crowded canyon

of hungry and ravenous
14th street.

mister raisins

mister raisins
has all of the plastic bags
left in new york city
piled up next to him
on the R train

he goes through them
pulling out pairs of socks and pants
t-shirts and collared ones

moving them from one bag to another

occasionally he pulls out
a small box of raisins
from one of the bags

and puts it in his pocket
like he's found a secret treat

mister raisins
has beer cans and sunscreen
in his plastic bags

sneakers and winter gloves

a corduroy coat that he keeps
in a big, red plastic bag
braced between his legs

he takes it out and looks at it
then puts it back in the bag

but not before
pulling out another small box of raisins

no one seems to care about him

but mister raisins
is the most fascinating person to me
on the R train

he's better
than the manhattan skyline
the statue of liberty
and the new world trade center

the dull women in short skirts
playing on their cell phones

the brooklyn bridge
or the guy in the danzig t-shirt

with the unkempt hair
and crazy eyes

the one who keeps shouting about
how he's the new savior

how he's bigger than god
the president
or even jesus christ.

red buckets

it is
almost passable for warm
in mid november

so they are out there like clockwork

the two of them
dueling idiots

with their red buckets
washing their cars

the one will wash and wipe down a side
then stand back to admire it
like he just bought a van gogh

the other blasts rap music
to compensate for his age

driving me
and the rabid dogs
crazy with the noise of bass

showing his fat ass
to impressionable senile old women
as he really works to gloss his rims

these are men of small minds
and no tangible imagination

they fill their void with nonsense like cars
and independence day and the super bowl

they are tepid wet dreams

sudsy red buckets
of horseshit
and very little else.

lone cheer from the sidewalk
for the pissed off pigeon
while casually forgetting
that millions of people go hungry each day
--after Richard Hugo

he grabs for morsels
he is choking down life

it is raining again
and the weather here
has no clue about the holiday season

new york city is nothing but a postcard
for television and tourists
this time of year

and i am depressed without end
at the coming of another decade

if i make it
i will see myself become an old man

with old man ideals that have nothing left to burn

not that this pigeon cares
walking angrily in a circle

tossing lost bagel into the sky
like a cat toying with a trapped mouse

there are more visceral needs
than paying attention to the existential malaise
of another well-fed white man on the street

making comfortable bargains
with father time

like getting bits of food in your mouth
before another pigeon comes along

dodging taxis
and little prick children

or wondering
when this is all over

where your next good meal
is coming from.

homeless quilt

the cops are smiling
on facebook

beefy knuckleheads
who haven't read a book
except to throw one at you
for some trumped-up bullshit

they are holding up
a group of taped together cardboard signs

a homeless "quilt" they call it in their post

signs they took from people
panhandling on the streets during christmas

one sign says

homeless
need help
thank you &
god bless

another says

trying to make it
anything helps
god bless

there are seven to eight more like it
all bunched together

and the cops in the picture
are smiling their cops smiles
while dressed in their little cop uniforms

they look well-fed
like they've never missed a meal

never not had a roof over their heads
or someone else to wipe their asses

or been stuck on the street
any longer than it takes
to order a cup of coffee

catch their little cop reflection
in a rearview mirror

before marching off to hassle
another broken someone

whom america has gone
and let down again.

winter, it's sixty-six degrees
in january in new york city

the basketball boys
are wearing sweat shorts

and smell like marijuana
coming back from the park

they hustle fast words
at girls wearing jeans
with one hundred-dollar rips in the thighs

in union square
people stroll the farmers market
sit on benches eating ice cream cones

walk their dogs
looking like happy suicides

even the climate scientists have given up
and are eating falafel over rice
in washington square park

winter, it's sixty-six degrees
in january in new york city

and every dumb smile
looks like death

like an apocalypse

as, overdressed,
i wipe the sweat off of my brow

watch two pigeons
fight over a slice of pizza

look down an avenue
of big buildings bowing in the sun

toward a rising river
of swirling garbage and oil

that'll most likely
flood and murder me one day.

the car honker

the car honker outside
keeps slamming on the horn

someone has blocked him in
and he's pissed

normally, i would try and empathize

but i've worked six days
without a break
as a public servant

i have had too many nights like this here

too many car honkers
and other assorted and loud assholes

i go to my window
and tell him to keep it down

the car honker looks at me and says,
why don't you go and fuck off too, bitch?

and i look at him
with both fists clinched

head over to get my coat and shoes
and the thick stick of a broom

thinking empathy and understanding
can go and walk a fucking marathon

tonight.

mike the pilot drinks at the catch-22 bar

his face is cherub red
and pock-marked

a w.c. fields tribute of abuse

his belly has grown
to a tank of cheap beer

it's been eleven years
many a blurry night between us

but i recognize him anyway

even if he's not clad
in a white short-sleeved shirt

with those striped patches on his shoulders
the wings pinned crooked on his breast

all day on the new york to chicago run
all evening taking up a stool at rooney's pub

soused enough to make me think twice
about every commercial flight i took

mike the pilot drinks
at the catch-22 bar

with a woman who looks
twenty years younger than him

looks disappointed and bored
as she sits there picking at a bowl of pretzels

watching his head bob up and down

a man starving for slumber
more than conversation and alcohol

like mike was never the man
who took mona on the men's room sink

and made her cum so hard
that it broke right off its hinges
and cracked in half

on the sticky, piss-stained floor

mike the pilot
looks old and useless

sitting there in the catch-22
with his beer untouched

all of the action and adventure
drained right out of him

the years gone from blessings into a curse
as the woman he's with
gets up to play a song on the jukebox

a classic one from back
when mike was young and virile

when the booze flowed like rivers
the uniform was animal magnetism

and the bright, blue sky
was likely everything to him

except the limit.

men standing outside the catch-22 bar

the boozy semi-circle
of domestic light beer vapor
and cigarette smoke

their shambling silhouettes
dancing against the streetlights

the sputtering violence of words

it's obvious these men
aren't discussing socrates

or china's role
in southeast asian policy

again tonight

the homeless guy outside of my job
doesn't care about our little pandemic

he
needs
to use the bathroom

and if we're closed
he'll scream and rant and rave

stick his hand down his pants
come up with an armful of shit
and smear it on our door

claim the dog did it
as he runs away from the cops

the homeless guy outside of my job
doesn't care about our little pandemic

or washing his hands
for twenty seconds
while he hums the ABCs

or where he can get some hand sanitizer
and rubber gloves

how many people are infected
how many people have died

whether or not
the president is incompetent

he wants to use the shitter now
find a place to sleep now

and if he can't get that?

then he's content
to spread his feces
like a master baker

all over the glass and door handle

cackling
at our outrage
wide enough

so that we can see his one good tooth
in the thick, brown smear

as he stumbles away

a big, dirty infection
a capitalist plague

the original global virus.

eating a cheeseburger during the end times

the bar has
most of its televisions
turned to Fox business channel

except for one playing
a mets/nationals game
from last year

the men in the bar
are watching the stock market crash

again and again

with as rapt attention
as they would ESPN

tomorrow the world is on lockdown

and this bar will be closed
like thousands of others

while we wait out the pandemic

but today is for eating a cheeseburger
during the end times

as men in the bar complain about the money
they'll lose on the stock market
instead of maybe losing their health or their lives

men seem to worry
about the most trivial of things
in times of crsis

a week ago i was complaining about my job

yesterday i fought two people
for the last loaf of bread

and screamed into the void about the lack
of toilet paper and black beans

and who in the hell knows
if i'll have a job to go back to

i probably should be indoors
making neighborly peace and hand sanitizing my soul

binge-watching a world
that now looks so foreign to me

but they make a damned good cheeseburger here

and it might be months, if ever,
before i get to have it again

the bartender, ross, is losing his job tomorrow
he just took a bath on his disney stock an hour ago

and got a text that his fiancé lost her job right now
they were planning for a wedding in may

the unraveling is happening in real time
and there is nothing to do or say

but just sit here and wait on it

except for some guy in a FDNY t-shirt
who says…the flu killed more people yesterday

everyone laughs
and nods silently

they go back to watching
the stock market crash on tv

sucking up a trillion in government money

as i clear my second beer
and turn to the year old mets/nationals game

cheering when Juan Soto hits a double

a fool move for sure

but forgetting
forgetting all of this
if only for a moment.

barney sits outside the indigo tavern

barney sits
outside the indigo tavern
like it's going to open any minute

he sits on the wooden bench
that he's usually on

smoking his unfiltered cigarettes

he sits there
like there's a new pint
waiting for him inside

and a mets game on the tv

like phil is in there with his cheap scotch
dennis with his cheap white wine and ice cubes

barney sits there smiling
like he's got a joke to tell darlene

if he's lucky
he'll flirt with jill

barney sits outside
checking his watch

but the indigo has been closed for three months
as the pandemic raged on and on

the american flags outside the bar
are yellow and drooping

tattered at their fringes

no one planted new flowers
in the big stone plots

bill caught the covid from watching Fox News
and dennis is afraid to come outside

darlene says that stimulus check
didn't do her for shit
and the unemployment
barely lets her slide by

barney sits
outside the indigo tavern
on a bright sunny day in june

waiting like he always does

as a truck full of day laborers
pull up to the curb
and get out of a big red truck

they have ladders
and tool boxes with them
saws and big planks of wood

a new padlock
a for rent sign

and the bright brass keys
to the indigo's classic front door.

John Grochalski is the author of the poetry collections, *The Noose Doesn't Get Any Looser After You Punch Out* (Six Gallery Press 2008), *Glass City* (Low Ghost Press, 2010), *In The Year of Everything Dying* (Camel Saloon, 2012), *Starting with the Last Name Grochalski* (Coleridge Street Books, 2014), and *The Philosopher's Ship* (Alien Buddha Press, 2018). He is also the author of the novels, *The Librarian* (Six Gallery Press 2013), and *Wine Clerk* (Six Gallery Press 2016). Grochalski currently lives in Brooklyn, New York.

BLACK DRAGON POETRY SOCIETY
CERTIFIED AND APPROVED